Teaching With

Dear Canada

Build Important Social Studies and Language Skills with Historical Fiction

by
Amy von Heyking

■SCHOLASTIC
Teaching
Resources

Scholastic Canada Ltd.

Table of Contents

For information on the complete Dear Canada series and on the value of using historical fiction to teach social studies, go to www.scholastic.ca/dearcanada

A Timeline of Canadian History..3

The Death of My Country: The Plains of Abraham Diary of Geneviève Aubuchon
Summary/What's Going On in the World in 1759? 6
Prior Knowledge/Discussion Questions 7
Extended Activities 12
Reproducibles 14
Bibliography 16

A Rebel's Daughter: The 1837 Rebellion Diary of Arabella Stevenson
Summary/What's Going On in the World in 1837 and 1838? 17
Prior Knowledge/Discussion Questions 18
Extended Activities 23
Reproducibles 24
Bibliography 26

No Safe Harbour: The Halifax Explosion Diary of Charlotte Blackburn
Summary/What's Going On in the World in 1917 and 1918? 27
Prior Knowledge/Discussion Questions 28
Extended Activities 33
Reproducibles 34
Bibliography 36

Turned Away: The World War II Diary of Devorah Bernstein
Summary/What's Going On in the World in 1941 and 1942? 37
Prior Knowledge/Discussion Questions 38
Extended Activities 41
Reproducibles 43
Bibliography 45

Activities for General Use 46

A Timeline of Canadian History

About 18,000 B.C.	The first inhabitants of North America probably cross from Siberia via a land bridge.
About A.D. 1001	Leif Ericsson makes his first voyage to Vinland.
1497	John Cabot makes the first of two voyages for England to the fishing grounds of Newfoundland.
1534	Jacques Cartier claims the Gaspé peninsula for France. The following year he travels up the St. Lawrence to Stadacona (now Québec City) and Hochelaga (now Montréal) and names the territory "Canada."
1576	Martin Frobisher makes the first of three journeys to find the Northwest Passage.
1583	Sir Humphrey Gilbert claims Newfoundland for England.
1604	Samuel de Champlain establishes a colony at Nova Scotia.
1608	Champlain establishes a permanent French colony at Québec.
1615	The first Roman Catholic missionaries attempt to convert aboriginal people to Christianity.
1642	The founding of Montréal.
1649	The Iroquois complete the destruction of the Huron nation and begin to raid French settlements.
1663	Jean Talon is appointed Intendant of New France. King Louis XIV commits to defending the colony and promoting settlement.
1670	The British crown grants a charter to the Hudson's Bay Company.
1713	The Treaty of Utrecht.
1749	The British establish Halifax.
1755	The British begin the expulsion of the Acadians.
1756-1763	The Seven Years War between Britain and France, during which the British capture Louisbourg (1758) and Québec in the battle of the Plains of Abraham (1759), and the French surrender New France to the British (1760).
1759	***The Death of My Country***
1769	Prince Edward Island becomes a colony of Great Britain.
1774	The passage of the Québec Act.
1776	The creation of the North West Company.
1778	Captain James Cook explores the Pacific Coast.
1775–1783	The American Revolutionary War, during which the Thirteen Colonies gain independence from Great Britain. The people of Québec, Nova Scotia and Prince Edward Island remain loyal to Great Britain. About 40,000 Loyalists from the Thirteen Colonies join them.

1791	Québec is divided into two separate colonies: Lower and Upper Canada.
1792	Captain George Vancouver makes the first of three voyages to explore Vancouver Island and the coast of British Columbia.
1793	Explorer Alexander Mackenzie crosses the Rocky and Coastal Mountains to reach the Pacific Ocean.
1793	John Graves Simcoe establishes York (now Toronto) on the shore of Lake Ontario.
1811	The first group of Lord Selkirk's settlers arrives at Hudson Bay.
1812–1815	The War of 1812, between Great Britain and the United States, in which Isaac Brock is killed (Battle of Queenston Heights in 1812), Laura Secord becomes a hero (1813) and Tecumseh dies (1813).
1837	***A Rebel's Daughter***
1837	Rebellions in Upper and Lower Canada result in a visit from Lord Durham and the recommendation that the colonies should receive responsible government.
1841	The Act of Union unites Upper and Lower Canada into the Province of Canada.
1843	Victoria is established on Vancouver Island.

1851	Canada's first postage stamp is issued. It has only been possible to send mail overseas for about ten years.
1857	Ottawa becomes the new capital of Canada.
1858	British Columbia becomes a colony of Great Britain when gold is discovered in the Fraser River.
1867	The British North America Act is passed. New Brunswick, Nova Scotia, Québec and Ontario form the Dominion of Canada.
1869	The Métis in the Red River region rebel when Canada purchases the territory from the Hudson's Bay Company.
1870	The province of Manitoba joins Confederation. The Northwest Territories are created.
1871	British Columbia joins Confederation.
1873	The Cypress Hills massacre results in the creation of the North West Mounted Police to keep order in the new territories.
1873	Prince Edward Island joins Confederation.
1885	The Métis of the Northwest Territories rebel against the Canadian government. Their leader, Louis Riel, is later hanged.
1885	The last spike of the main line of the Canadian Pacific Railway is

driven at Craigellachie, British Columbia.

1896   Gold is discovered in the Klondike.

1898   Yukon becomes a federal territory.

1899–1902   Canadians fight for the British during the Boer War in South Africa.

1905   Saskatchewan and Alberta join Confederation.

1914–1918   Britain declares war on Germany. Canada participates as part of the British Empire.

1917   ***No Safe Harbour***

1917   The Halifax explosion.

1918   Women are granted the right to vote in federal elections.

1919   The Winnipeg general strike.

1927   The first coast-to-coast radio broadcast in Canada.

1929   The Persons Case.

1929   The stock market crash of October 29 marks the beginning of the Great Depression.

1936   The establishment of the Canadian Broadcasting Corporation.

1939–45   Canada participates in the Second World War.

1941   ***Turned Away***

1947   The oil strike at Leduc No. 1 in Alberta marks the beginning of the province's oil boom.

1949   Newfoundland joins Confederation.

1960   Aboriginal people living on reserves are granted the right to vote in federal elections.

1965   Canada adopts a new flag featuring a red maple leaf.

1970   The FLQ, a terrorist group attempting to establish an independent Québec through revolution, kidnaps a British trade commissioner and a Québec cabinet minister. The federal government, under Prime Minister Pierre Trudeau, invokes the War Measures Act.

1982   The Constitution Act is passed, along with the Canadian Charter of Rights and Freedoms.

1989   The North American Free Trade Agreement comes into effect.

1999   Nunavut is created as a federal territory.

THE DEATH OF MY COUNTRY

THE PLAINS OF ABRAHAM DIARY OF GENEVIÈVE AUBUCHON

QUÉBEC, NEW FRANCE, 1759

by Maxine Trottier

Summary: Geneviève and her brother Chegual are Alnanbal (Abenaki) children who were taken in by a French couple at Québec after the destruction of their village and people. By 1759 Chegual has returned to life with the Abenaki, but Geneviève has found a home with Mme Claire and been educated by the Ursuline nuns at Québec. As rumours fly about the impending attack by the British, Geneviève refuses to go to the Abenaki St. Francis mission with her brother. Instead they stay and, together with their friend Étienne, endure the siege of Québec. When the British win the Battle of the Plains of Abraham, they also endure occupation by British troops and the martial law they impose. As the British and the French Canadians recover in the aftermath of the battle, they learn about each other and come to appreciate how much they have in common.

What's Going On in the World in 1759?

- Scottish poet Robert Burns is born.
- Composer Georg Frideric Handel dies in London.
- The volcano Vesuvius erupts in Italy.
- French philosopher Voltaire writes the novel *Candide*.
- The British Museum opens in London.

——• Prior Knowledge •——

The Historical Note at the end of the diary gives some background information about the Seven Years War, sometimes described as the world's first global war. It was fought between Britain, Prussia and Hanover on one side against France, Austria, Sweden, Saxony, Russia and Spain on the other. Battles were in Europe, India and the Caribbean as well as North America. Students should complete a timeline or have some understanding of the events in all of these regions between 1756 and 1763 to better put this story in historical context. During this war, Britain did not fight in Europe, instead concentrating on conquering France's colonies and destroying its navy.

Hostilities between the British and the French began in North America in 1754, but Britain did not declare war against France until 1756. This war in North America is also called the French and Indian War, referring to the two enemies of Britain in this conflict — France and its First Nations allies such as the Algonquin, Wyandot, Ojibwa, and Mi'kmaq. Students could discuss whether this is an appropriate name for the war since the Iroquois Confederacy was in fact allied with Britain in this conflict. A chronology of the events in North America is provided at the end of the diary. During the negotiations to end the war, France considered demanding the return of Canada, but in the end opted to concede Britain's claim on the conquered territory and instead demanded the return of Guadeloupe to its empire. The Treaty of Paris (1763) left France with the small islands of St. Pierre and Miquelon in the Gulf of St. Lawrence as its only possessions north of the Caribbean.

A French Canadian militiaman

In order to build students' background knowledge, teachers may find it useful to use the reference materials listed in the bibliography on page 16 in order to prepare brief research packages on topics such as: Abenaki culture; the government of New France; everyday life in New France; Marie Guyart de l'Incarnation and the Ursulines; and life as a soldier. Students could be divided into "expert" groups to review these materials and then, using a jigsaw strategy, could be regrouped to teach others about their area of expertise.

——• Discussion Questions •——

Before commencing the reading, ask students questions that will help them make some personal connections to the major themes in the diary, such as:

• Talk or write about a time that you felt torn between two people. What did you do?

• Write about a time when you misjudged someone. What were your first impressions? How did you discover that you were mistaken? What did you do after?

- Are there people in your community who might feel torn between two cultures? How would this happen? How might they cope? (There may be a story in the news, for example, about recent immigrants to Canada coping with a new culture and environment.)

Comment on the first entry in the diary. Is it an effective opening? How does the author grab your attention?

How do we know that Geneviève has two "identities"? What are they? (pp. 3-4)

What do you think a "totem" is? Why is a small bird Geneviève's totem?

Who do you think Chegual is?

Do you think most girls at this time would be able to read and write? How does the author account for Geneviève's ability to read and write? Is this realistic? (pp. 4-5)

Mère Esther tells Geneviève that it is good that her life is ordinary. What does she mean by that?

Why doesn't Geneviève know her real age (pp. 5-7)? What is a *voyageur*? What is a surgeon apothecary? What kinds of things do you imagine Chegual found difficult about living with Mme Claire and M. Jacques? About attending the seminary?

Why would thirty-two books be a considerable library for a home at this time? (p. 7)

With the information you have so far, begin a character map that shows the relationship of everyone in Geneviève's family and household. (p. 9)

Why is bread becoming so expensive for the household? What other household items do you think might be rising in price or becoming difficult to acquire? (pp. 10-11)

What does it mean to be "cloistered"? (p. 12)

What does Geneviève have in common with Mme Claire and with Mère Esther?

Why doesn't Geneviève pull the weeds in the herb garden? (p. 13)

Draw a sketch of Chegual based on Geneviève's description.

Why is the little rabbit called Wigwedi? (pp. 14-15)

☙ Why is Étienne's greeting to Geneviève brazen? (p. 17)

☙ Why did Étienne choose to live among the Abenaki? (p. 18)

☙ Why do think the Abenaki are banned from the town at night? (p. 29)

☙ Draw a quick sketch of Geneviève's special outfit for the dinner. (p. 35)

☙ Do you think Geneviève should go with Chegual to the Abenaki mission at St. Francis? (pp. 39-40)

☙ On what date do the residents of Québec hear that the British ships are near (p. 45)? Begin a timeline of the siege of Québec beginning with this date and adding other major events mentioned throughout the diary.

☙ Geneviève brings medicine to the nuns at the Ursuline convent and to the Abenaki children at the encampment (pp. 47-52). Where do you think she learned about healing and the medicine in plants?

☙ Why is Geneviève so troubled by her visit to the Abenaki encampment? (pp. 49-52)

☙ Why has Geneviève decided to remain in the town? (p. 61)

☙ Do you think Geneviève is ashamed of her tattoos? Why or why not? (pp. 62-63)

☙ How does Étienne feel about Geneviève? What evidence can you identify to support your answer?

☙ Draw a quick sketch of Geneviève in the Abenaki clothing (pp. 63-64). How does it make her feel?

☙ Who do you think is the officer Geneviève sees through her telescope (p. 70)? Is this a realistic event to include in the diary? Why do you think the author included this?

☙ The "Rangers" Geneviève refers to on page 72 of the diary are Rogers' Rangers, an independent company of soldiers attached to the British Army at this time. Do some research about them to discover how they were formed and what contributions they made to the British victory in the French and Indian War.

☙ Why did the men in the merchants' detachment panic so easily (pp. 76-77)? Write a brief newspaper advertisement encouraging men to join.

☙ How do the people of Québec react to the bombardment? What do they do to try to keep safe? (pp. 80-83)

ᔥ Why might a Canadian couple give aid and comfort to the British forces? (pp. 84-5)

ᔥ What is a gibbet? Why would General Montcalm order the execution of two of his own soldiers? (p. 86)

ᔥ Who might the "men who wear skirts" be? What were they carrying past the French soldiers? (p. 87)

ᔥ Who are the soldiers in skirts? What does Chegual mean when he says they fight like Abenaki, not like the British? (pp. 89-90)

ᔥ The Basse-Ville was destroyed by August 10. How long has the siege of Québec been going on? (p. 93)

Montcalm riding along the French lines before the battle

ᔥ Why would the British burn the farmland around Québec?

ᔥ Read Geneviève's entry for 13 September until the passage, "It is your choice, ma chère." The British army is on the heights above the town and Chegual wants to take his sister to St. Francis. Should she go? (pp. 100-101)

ᔥ Why does Étienne think Geneviève should stay in Québec? How does he convince Chegual to stay and fight the British on the heights? (pp. 102-103)

Wolfe leading his army at the battle of the Plains of Abraham

ᔥ How realistic is it that Geneviève left the house to watch the Battle of the Plains of Abraham (pp. 103-105)? Is there any other way the author could have included this information in the diary?

ᔥ How might you find out if the Marquis de Montcalm really died in the apothecary's house in Québec on September 14? (pp. 107-109)

ᔥ Why would they bury Montcalm in secret? (pp. 109-110)

ᔥ Québec surrenders to the British on September 18. How long was the siege?

ᔥ Why is Geneviève so angry with Intendant Bigot? What does "hoarding" mean? (p. 112)

✑ What do you think has happened to Étienne and Chegual?

✑ Is Geneviève right to refuse to nurse the British and their allies? (p. 114)

✑ What do you think the injured Scottish soldier said to Geneviève? (p. 120)

✑ Why do Mme Claire and Mère Esther pity Geneviève for her refusal to help the Scottish soldier? Why do you think she does help with the amputation? (pp. 123-126)

Montcalm, mortally wounded on the Plains of Abraham, being taken back to Quebec

✑ What does Mme Claire mean by a scarred heart? What do you think Geneviève is going to confess to her priest? (p. 127)

✑ The rules the British imposed on the Canadians were not much harsher than those in place before the Conquest. Why is Geneviève so angry about those rules? (p. 131)

✑ Why would General Murray allow the Canadians, and even those Scots under his command, to continue to practise their Roman Catholic faith? (pp. 132-133)

✑ What part of her past is Geneviève trying to bury? (p. 134)

✑ What language do the Scots speak to each other? (p. 140)

✑ Why is Lieutenant Doig writing his account of the war in French? (pp. 142-143)

✑ Geneviève says that "everything is changed" after she reads Lieutenant Doig's diary. What does she mean by that? (pp. 142-144)

✑ What should Geneviève's penance be? (p. 145)

✑ In what ways might Lieutenant Knox's account of the war be different than Doig's? (p. 146)

✑ Why would Chegual and Doig become friends? (pp. 146-150)

✑ Why does the meal result in conflict between Geneviève and Doig? (pp. 152-153)

◌ What was Étienne's "message" for Geneviève? Why does it bring her such relief? (pp. 158-159)

◌ What evidence is there by the end of the diary that Geneviève will in fact be able to put the past behind her? (p. 168)

◌ Before reading the Epilogue, predict what will happen to Geneviève and her friends and family.

◌ After reading the Epilogue, decide if you think this is a good ending. What do you think should have happened to Geneviève and the others?

◌ The title of the diary is *The Death of My Country*. Do you think this is an accurate title? In what way(s) did Geneviève's country die? Can you think of another title for the diary that reflects her feelings at the end?

—— Extended Activities ——

• Throughout the diary, keep a list of the characters you think were real people. Check to see if you are correct and then do some research to find out more about them. Some historical figures that the author includes or mentions are:

— Marie de l'Incarnation
— Esther Wheelwright
— Louis-Antoine de Bougainville
— François Bigot
— Pierre de Rigaud, Marquis de Vaudreuil
— James Wolfe
— Louis-Joseph, Marquis de Montcalm
— Simon Fraser (of the 78th Fraser Highlanders)

• Keep a timeline of the major events in the siege of Québec as recorded by Geneviève. Include:

— The people of Québec first discover that the British are on the river and on their way to Québec.
— The Canadian militia is called up.
— British warships arrive at Québec.
— The British establish an encampment near Chutes-Montmorency.
— The British begin to attack Québec.
— Montcalm dies.
— Québec surrenders to the British.
— Montréal falls to the British.

- Write a newspaper account of the beginning of the siege of Québec, described by Geneviève on pp. 80-82.

- Compare and contrast Geneviève's account of the Battle of the Plains of Abraham with those found in the non-fiction resources included in the bibliography on page 16. How did the author incorporate historical facts into Geneviève's account?

Wolfe's warships approaching French entrenchments near Montmorency Falls

- Many times during the diary Geneviève comments on the barbarity of warfare. She also mentions the truces and other "rules" soldiers seem to abide by during the conflict. Use the T-chart reproducible on page 14. On one side, record instances she mentions of the brutality of the warfare of this historical period. Provide a direct quote from the diary as evidence. On the other side, record the evidence she provides for the rules the soldiers and commanders seem to abide by. Again, provide a direct quote for each instance you record.

- Create a Venn diagram that compares and contrasts the French Canadians and the Abenaki. Add another circle for the Scots if you like.

- The plot of any story is driven by conflict, a struggle between forces. In the case of this diary, the plot revolves around the external conflict of the British and the French in Québec. The plot, however, also revolves around Geneviève's internal conflict, a conflict she feels inside herself. Use the reproducible on page 15 to record evidence from the diary that demonstrates these conflicts, and the resolutions the author creates.

- On pages 9 and 10 of the diary Geneviève "counts" the happiness in her life in several interesting ways. How might she "count" her happiness at the end of the diary?

- Geneviève often writes about her Abenaki as well as her French (Canadian) identity. Her husband Andrew is proud of his French as well as his Scottish roots. Using the Gaelic motto that Geneviève repeats to her family in the Epilogue, design a family crest for Geneviève and Andrew's children.

Name _____

Two Faces of War

Support each example with a quote from the diary.

Cruelty of War	Civility of War

Name _____

Conflicts Within and Without

Conflict =
a struggle between forces.

Geneviève's Internal Conflict	External Conflict: Battle of the Plains of Abraham
Quote:	Quote:

Resolution	Resolution
Quote:	Quote:

THE DEATH OF MY COUNTRY
THE PLAINS OF ABRAHAM DIARY OF GENEVIÈVE AUBUCHON

—•— Bibliography —•—

Non-fiction

Baldwin, Douglas. (2003). *Revolution, War and the Loyalists*. Calgary: Weigl Educational Publishers.

Gillis, Jennifer B. (2003). *Life in New France*. Chicago: Heinemann.

Livesey, Robert, & Smith, A.G. (2003). *New France*. Markham, ON: Fitzhenry & Whiteside Publishing.

Maestro, Betsy. (2000). *Struggle for a Continent: The French and Indian Wars 1689-1763*. New York: HarperCollins Publishers.

Fiction

Bruchac, Marg. (2005). *Malian's Song*. Middlebury, VT: Vermont Folklife Center.

Bruchac, Joseph. (1995). *Dog People: Native Dog Stories*. Golden, CO: Fulcrum Publishing.

Bruchac, Joseph. (2002). *Winter People*. New York: Dial Books.

Downie, Mary Alice. (2000). *Danger in Disguise*. Montréal: Roussan Publishers.

Background Information for Teachers

Baker, C. Alice. (2006). *True Stories of New England Captives: Carried to Canada During the Old French and Indian Wars*. Kessinger Publishing LLC.

Borneman, Walter. (2006). *The French and Indian War: Deciding the Fate of North America*. New York: HarperCollins Publishers.

Brumwell, Stephen. (2002). *Redcoats: The British Soldier and War in America, 1755-1763*. Cambridge: Cambridge University Press.

Carroll, Joy. (2004). *Wolfe and Montcalm: Their Lives, Their Times and the Fate of a Continent*. Richmond Hill, ON: Firefly Books.

Dale, Ronald J. (2004). *The Fall of New France: How the French Lost a North American Empire*. Toronto: James Lorimer & Company.

LaPierre, Laurier. (1990). *1759: The Battle for Canada*. Toronto: McClelland and Stewart.

Stacey, Charles P. & Graves, Donald E. (2002). *Québec, 1759: The Siege and the Battle*. Rev. ed. Toronto: Robin Brass Studio.

Wiseman, Frederick M. (2001). *The Voice of the Dawn: An Autohistory of the Abenaki Nation*. Hanover, NH: University Press of New England.

Websites

http://1759.ccbn-nbc.gc.ca
—1759: From the Warpath to the Plains of Abraham (Virtual Museum), created by the North American Battlefield Commission; an interactive, virtual exhibit

http://www.ccbn-nbc.gc.ca/_en/batailles
—Government of Canada, National Battlefields Commission, Plains of Abraham; a description of the battles of 1759-60

TV documentary

Wheelwright Ink Ltd. (2005). *Captive: the Story of Esther*. 48 minutes.

The story of Esther Wheelwright, abducted by the Abenaki from her New England home and brought to Québec. She converted to Roman Catholicism and became an Ursuline nun and eventually Mother Superior of the order. The film is distributed by THA Media, 175 Bloor St. E., Suite 610, Toronto, Ontario, M4W 3R8

(416) 925-3766 (phone)

(416) 925-3116 (fax)

A Rebel's Daughter
The 1837 Rebellion Diary of Arabella Stevenson

Toronto, Upper Canada, 1837

by Janet Lunn

Summary: It is December 1837 and Arabella Stevenson is worried about her father who has been arrested for participating in the rebellion against the government of Upper Canada. With her brother gone and her mother unwilling to take responsibility for her family, Arabella must arrange for the sale of her family's home and possessions. Soon her life of ease and privilege disappears, she is rejected by former friends and she is forced to take the job of a scullery maid in the home of one of her former schoolmates, Elizabeth Harvard. Her family background and education, however, make it difficult for the other servants in the household to accept her. She is truly isolated and alone. The difficulty and drudgery of the work do not keep her from worrying about the fate of her father and the other rebels. As the months pass, some of the rebels are tried and hanged. Others, including Arabella's father, are sentenced to be transported to the British penal colony of Van Diemen's Land. But when relatives in England give Arabella and her mother the opportunity to move to England, Arabella refuses, preferring to stay in Upper Canada, even if she has to live and work as a servant. But her future will not consist of scullery work. While working in the Harvard household she befriends their grandmother who hires her to be her full-time companion and offers her the opportunity to continue the education she began. As she begins her new life as a companion, she no longer mourns the wealth and life she lost; she appreciates the true friends she has found and the gifts she has been given.

What's Going On in the World in 1837 and 1838?

- Victoria becomes Queen of the British Empire at 18.
- Gabriel Dumont, a leader of the Métis, is born at Red River, now Winnipeg.
- The world's first kindergarten opens in Germany.
- In Illinois, blacksmith John Deere invents a steel plow for heavy prairie sod.
- Installments of Charles Dickens' *Oliver Twist* appear in a British magazine.

—•— Prior Knowledge —•—

The Historical Note at the end of the diary gives some background information about the nature of the colonial government of Upper Canada, the goals of the reformers and the events of the Rebellion of 1837. Students may benefit from more detailed background information found in the resources listed in the bibliography on page 26. Since most of the diary covers the aftermath of the Rebellion in 1838, students will need more information about life in Toronto in this period for girls and for the poor in order to better appreciate the situation Arabella faces when her father is jailed.

Students could also consider the fate that awaited the convicted rebels. While only two rebels were hanged, twenty-five were sent to Van Diemen's Land, the British penal colony established in 1803, now part of Australia. They could do some research about the penal colony and its treatment of prisoners. They could listen to U2's song "Van Diemen's Land" (on the *Rattle and Hum* album) which is dedicated to the leader of an uprising against the British in Ireland in 1848.

—•— Discussion Questions —•—

Before commencing the reading, ask students questions that will help them make some predictions about the story.

• What kind of men participated in the Rebellion of 1837? Who were the leaders? What kinds of jobs did they have?

• What was the fate of the rebels after the rebellion?

• What might life have been like for their families?

• In what ways do you think the lives of girls were different in the 1830s?

✿Why would Arabella's mother object to her writing the word "burst" in her diary? (p. 3)

✿Why would the author use the word "gaol" rather than "jail"?

✿What is the difference between a rebel and a reformer? (p. 4)

✿What is a barrister?

Rebels drilling in North York in autumn, 1837

Based on Arabella's first diary entry, do you think she comes from a wealthy, a middle-class or a poor family? Why?

Why aren't the girls at Arabella's school talking to her? Why does Miss St. Clair ask her to leave the school? (pp. 5-7)

Who is in Arabella's family? Begin to sketch a family tree with the information Arabella provides. (pp. 7-9)

Who are Sophie, Mary and Peggy? (pp. 10-12)

Why does Arabella have such a difficult time imagining her father as a rebel?

Why doesn't Arabella's mother want her to be friendly with the servants? What kind of person is her mother? (pp. 12-13)

Arrival of government supporters at the Parliament Buildings, Toronto, December 1837

Draw a quick sketch of the gaol as Arabella describes it. (pp. 13-15)

Where do you think Charlie is? (p. 16)

Compare and contrast Arabella's account of the events of December 5 and 6 with a non-fiction account. How has the author incorporated real events into Arabella's story? (pp. 17-23)

Where did Charlie go that night?

Who are the Family Compact? Why are Arabella's father and his friends so unhappy with them? Why would Arabella ask Mr. Jenkins about them, rather than her father? (pp. 26-28)

What evidence is there that Arabella's family is rich? What do you think is going to happen to them? (pp. 30-31)

Again, compare and contrast Arabella's version of the battle at Montgomery's Tavern with historians' accounts. How has the author incorporated real information in her story? What has she added and why? (pp. 31-34)

How long has Charlie been missing? Why is Arabella angry with her papa? (pp. 34-36)

۩ What do you think "parlous" means? Why is Arabella's family now poor? (pp. 36-39)

۩ Who do you think is more of a mother to Arabella — her real mother or Sophie? Why? (pp. 39-41)

The Battle of Montgomery's Farm

۩ Arabella says she isn't brave. Do you agree? How would you describe her behaviour as she meets with Mr. Dewhurst and her mother? (pp. 41-44)

۩ What does Arabella mean when she says that she's "not in charity with Mama"? (pp. 44-45)

۩ What kinds of things were Arabella and her mother allowed to keep from their house? (pp. 46-48)

۩ Draw a quick sketch of Arabella and her mother's rooms in King Street based on Arabella's description. (pp. 50-51)

۩ Write the conversation Arabella and Sophie had as they said goodbye.

۩ Why does Arabella's mother refuse to accept what has happened to them? Why doesn't she understand that she cannot have a maid? (pp. 51-53)

۩ Predict what is the "last worst thing" that has happened to Arabella. (p. 53)

۩ Compare and contrast Arabella's family with the Dewhurst family. (pp. 54-62)

۩ What is the "last worst thing" that has happened to Arabella?

۩ What does a scullery maid do? Why does Arabella find the work so difficult? (pp. 64-66)

۩ Based on the information Arabella gives, write an advertisement for a scullery maid, listing duties as well as the qualities a good candidate should have.

۩ Why is Arabella now called Betty?

۩ Why can't Arabella visit Jenny and Anne Dewhurst? (pp. 67-69)

✍ What do you think Mrs. Dewhurst would have liked to say to Arabella's mother when she went with Arabella to pick up her few belongings at King Street?

✍ How are the rich and poor treated differently at church? Why? (p. 70)

✍ Draw the rooms that Arabella knows in the Harvard home. What does she see in this house that she didn't see in her own home on Lot Street? (pp. 70-73)

✍ Arabella describes the six members of the Harvard family and the seven servants that live in the house. Does Arabella "fit into" either group? What does she have in common with the Harvard family? What does she have in common with the servants? Why are members of both groups so hard on her? (pp. 73-81)

✍ List at least five questions that Arabella would ask Papa if she saw him.

✍ Arabella is very unhappy at the Harvards' home. But after spending time in the kitchen, thinking in front of the fire, she resolves to get her own life back. What do you think she means by that? (pp. 88-89)

✍ Who do you think is brewing coffee in the middle of the night? (p. 91)

✍ Why do Mrs. Parliament and Arabella get on so well? In what way(s) are they alike? (pp. 104-105)

✍ Why does Arabella find it so difficult to visit her father in gaol? (pp. 106-107)

✍ Why doesn't Arabella tell her father the truth about her mother, Charlie and her work as a scullery maid? Do you think she's right to keep this information from him? (pp. 108-111)

✍ What did Arabella learn about Sukey because of their fight? Have her feelings toward her changed? (pp. 114-117)

✍ Arabella likes stories about girls who are "bold and brave" and yet she doesn't think she's brave. What do you think? Is Arabella brave? (p. 125)

✍ Why might Sukey be such a difficult student for Arabella? (p. 128)

✍ Arabella finally discovers that her brother Charlie is alive. How long has it been since he disappeared? (p. 131)

✍ Why does Cook want Arabella to write a letter for her? (pp. 131-133)

ᴕ What has happened to Charlie? Why wouldn't he have contacted Arabella in the months since he left? (pp. 134-136)

ᴕ Why does Arabella tear up her first letter to Charlie? (pp. 139-140)

ᴕ Arabella is very depressed when she realizes that her fantasy that her father will be set free will not come true. Yet, she soon seems to be in better spirits. What makes her feel better? (pp. 141-145)

ᴕ What is Arabella's birthday gift to herself (pp. 148-149)? Make Arabella a birthday card.

ᴕ Why doesn't Arabella want to go to England? (pp. 151-152)

ᴕ Do you think Arabella made the right decision about staying in Upper Canada and staying with the Harvards? (pp. 153-156)

ᴕ In what way(s) was Arabella's afternoon tea with the Dewhurst girls out of the ordinary? (pp. 157-159)

ᴕ Should Arabella give Sukey one of her dresses? (p. 161)

ᴕ Why does Mrs. Parliament decide to employ Arabella full-time? What will Arabella's duties be?

ᴕ How will her life change? (pp. 161-164)

ᴕ Write Arabella's last conversation with her mother. (pp. 164-165)

ᴕ Compare and contrast Arabella's life at the end of the diary with her life at the beginning (in her home in Lot Street). How has she changed? List at least five specific things that she has learned in her life as "Betty" the scullery maid. (pp. 166-168)

ᴕ Why is her August 13th entry her favourite in the diary?

ᴕ Before reading What Became of Them All, predict what will happen to Arabella and her friends and family.

ᴕ After reading the ending, decide if you think this is a good ending. What would you like to have happened to Arabella?

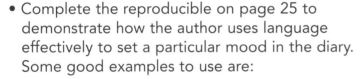

Extended Activities

- Throughout the diary, keep a list of the characters you think were real people. Check to see if you are correct and then do some research to find out more about them. Some historical figures that the author includes or mentions are:
  - William Lyon Mackenzie
  - John Strachan
  - Colonel James Fitzgibbon
  - Sir Francis Bond Head
  - Peter Matthews
  - Robert Baldwin
  - John Rolph
  - Samuel Lount
  - John George Lambton, Lord Durham

William Lyon Mackenzie

- Though this is subtitled *The 1837 Rebellion Diary*, most of the diary actually covers the year 1838 and describes the consequences of the rebellion for Arabella and the other members of the Stevenson family. Use the reproducible provided on page 24 to list the specific consequences of the rebellion for Arabella and other members of her family and household.

- Complete the reproducible on page 25 to demonstrate how the author uses language effectively to set a particular mood in the diary. Some good examples to use are:
  - Arabella describes the day her house and its contents are sold. (pp. 48-49)
  - Arabella spends the night outside her old house on Lot Street. (pp. 56-57)
  - Arabella spends her free Sunday afternoon walking and sitting by the lake. (pp. 122-123)

Sir Francis Bond Head

- Pretend you are Arabella. Write a letter persuading:
  - Justice John Beverley Robinson to have mercy on her father.
  - the government of Upper Canada to establish free schools for poor and working class children.
  - Bishop John Strachan to allow the poor and rich to sit together at church.
  - King's College to admit female students.

Name _____

Effects Web

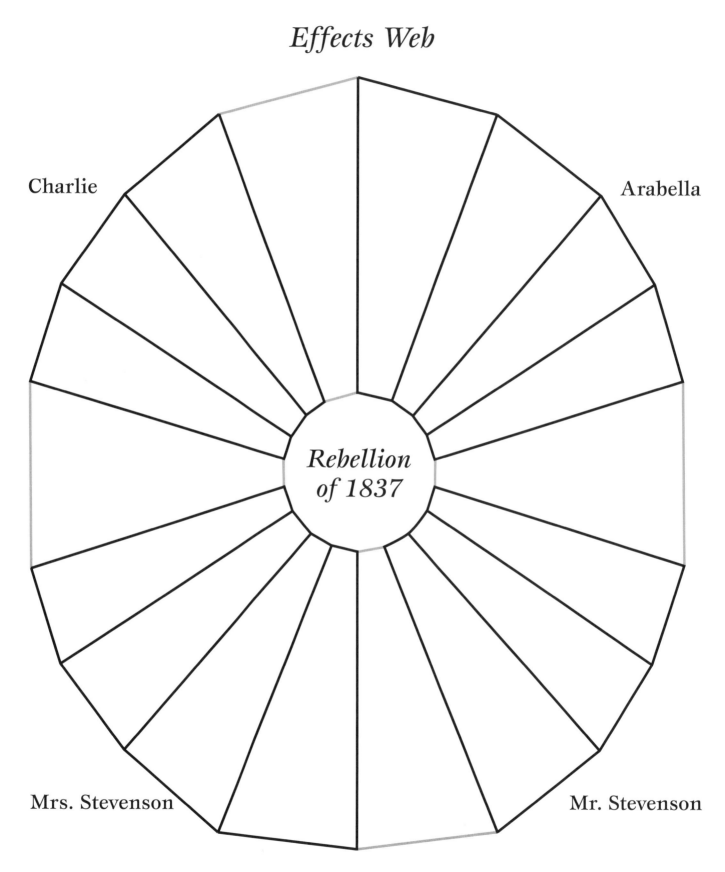

Charlie

Arabella

Rebellion
of 1837

Mrs. Stevenson

Mr. Stevenson

Name _____

Setting a Mood

Mood:

_____

_____

_____

_____

Words:

_____

_____

_____

_____

_____

Phrases:

_____

_____

_____

_____

_____

Sentences:

_____

_____

_____

_____

_____

_____

_____

_____

_____

_____

A Rebel's Daughter
The 1837 Rebellion Diary of Arabella Stevenson

— Bibliography —

Non-fiction

Baldwin, Douglas. (2003). *Rebellion and Union in the Canadas.* Calgary: Weigl Educational Publishers.

Cruxton, J. Bradley, Wilson, W. Douglas & Walker, Robert J. (2007). *Close-Up Canada.* 2nd ed. Toronto: Oxford University Press.

Mackay, Claire. (2002). *The Toronto Story.* Rev. ed. Toronto: Annick Press.

Quinlan, Don. (2005). *Rebellions.* Markham, ON: Fitzhenry & Whiteside Publishing.

Fiction

Brandis, Marianne. (1996). *Rebellion: A Novel of Upper Canada.* Erin, ON: Porcupine's Quill.

Crook, Connie Brummel. (2006). *Meyer's Rebellion.* Markham, ON: Fitzhenry & Whiteside Publishing.

Greenwood, Barbara. (1984). *A Question of Loyalty.* Toronto, ON: Scholastic Canada Ltd.

Background Information for Teachers

Careless, J.M.S. (1984). *Toronto to 1918.* Toronto: James Lorimer & Company.

Kilbourn, William & Stagg, Ronald. (2007). *The Firebrand: William Lyon Mackenzie and the Rebellion in Upper Canada.* Toronto: Dundurn Press.

Mackenzie, William Lyon. (1980). *Mackenzie's own narrative of the late rebellion, with illustrations and notes, critical and explanatory : exhibiting the only true account of what took place at the memorable siege of Toronto in the month of December, 1837.* Ottawa, ON: Golden Dog Press.

Prentice, Alison, et al. (1996). *Canadian Women: A History.* 2nd ed. Toronto: Harcourt Brace Canada.

Rooke, Patricia. (1983). *Discarding the Asylum: From Child Rescue to the Welfare State in English Canada, 1800 to 1950.* Lanham, MD: University Press of America.

Sewell, John. (2002). *Mackenzie: A Political Biography of William Lyon Mackenzie.* Toronto: James Lorimer & Company.

Websites

http://www.canadiana.org/citm/themes/constitution1_e
—Constitutional History section of "Canada in the Making" in Education on Early Canadiana on-line. There are detailed overviews of the political structure and history of Upper Canada from 1791 to 1837, and of the rebellion of 1837.

http://www.collectionscanada.gc.ca/confederation
—Library and Archives Canada, Collections Canada site on Confederation
The section called "Towards Confederation" has an excellent overview of the political history of Upper Canada, including the Rebellion of 1837 and its aftermath. The "People" section includes a biography of William Lyon Mackenzie.

TV documentary

Canadian Broadcasting Corporation. (2001). *Canada, A People's History,* Episode 7 (Rebellion and Reform 1815 – 1850)

No Safe Harbour

The Halifax Explosion Diary of Charlotte Blackburn

Halifax, Nova Scotia, 1917

by Julie Lawson

Summary: Charlotte's brother Luke is serving with the Canadian Army in France during World War I. For her twelfth birthday, he sends her a diary so she can record her life on the home front. For the first few weeks of her diary, her life is very much like any 12-year-old girl in Canada. She goes to school, visits with friends and neighbours and waits for word from her brother. She and her friends and family contribute to the war effort by knitting socks and rolling bandages. But everything changes on December 6, the day the munitions ship, the *Mont-Blanc*, collided with the *Imo*, resulting in a huge explosion and a tsunami that destroyed a large section of Halifax and left two thousand people dead and nine thousand injured. Charlotte's life is changed forever as she mourns the loss of family members and friends and, together with other survivors, tries to rebuild her life and community. But for Charlotte, the destruction of her family also means the discovery of other family members she thought long dead: her mother's parents. As she makes a new home with her grandparents she begins to cope with her losses and appreciate what remains.

What's Going On in the World in 1917 and 1918?

— Revolutions take place in Russia in February and October of 1917.

— Bread is rationed in Britain.

— Four women in the United States are jailed for picketing the White House in support of votes for women.

— World War I ends in November 1918.

— Spanish influenza kills over twenty million people worldwide.

— Women over 30 years of age are granted the vote in Britain.

— The New York Philharmonic Orchestra bans the performance of pieces by living German composers.

—•— **Prior Knowledge** —•—

The Historical Note at the end of the diary gives some background information about the importance of the port of Halifax, first settled by the British in 1749 as a military fortress. Students should understand the role Halifax played in World War I and the traffic the war brought to the port. They could examine photographs of Halifax and its harbour prior to the explosion to get a sense of the impact of the war on the community.

The Historical Note and accompanying maps and photographs also provide detailed information about the events of December 6, 1917. After reviewing the sequence of events leading to the explosion, students could debate whether the ultimate decision blaming both vessels for the explosion was correct.

Students should also be aware of the rescue and relief efforts that were made immediately after the explosion. They could discuss whether or not the city would have been able to cope with such a tragedy if so many soldiers and sailors had not been there. What did the city have to do to ensure that everyone's basic needs for food, clothing and shelter were met? How did Halifax cope with all the injured? Students should also examine photographs of the damaged areas of the city and of the rebuilding efforts.

Students could also do some prior research on issues or topics that come up in Charlotte's diary such as: life in the trenches; Canadians at Vimy and Passchendaele; conscription; women's work during the war; and war relief organizations such as the Junior Red Cross. Students could share their research as these topics are raised in the diary. They could also conduct research projects on these topics as an extension to the reading.

Damaged buildings on Gottingen Street; Fort Needham in the distance

—•— **Discussion Questions** —•—

Before commencing the reading, ask students questions that will help them make some predictions about the story.

• By 1917 Canada had been at war for several years. What was life like for the people in Canada? How did the war abroad affect the people on the home front?

The first entry in Charlotte's diary is a bit of a surprise. Do you think this is an effective opening? What does it tell us about Charlotte and her family? (pp. 3-4)

Use the information in Charlotte's first entry to begin a sketch of the Blackburn family tree. What other important information has Charlotte provided about her family? (pp. 5-8)

What does Charlotte's father do for a living? What else have we learned about her parents? (pp. 8-10)

What is a "balaclava helmet"? (p. 12)

Charlotte lives in Halifax, but what aspects of her life and neighbourhood sound more like life in the country? (pp. 10-13)

Why do you think Duncan is excited about joining the cadet corps? What do the boys in the corps do? (pp. 14-15)

Charlotte describes a letter Luke sends home describing his life at the front. If you were a soldier writing home would you want to tell your family how horrible your life is as a soldier, or would you hide the truth from them? Why? Find out what soldiers were and were not allowed to tell their families in their letters. Read some real letters home to see how they compare with those that Charlotte describes. (pp. 16-17)

Why does Charlotte feel bad that she used the word "Hun" to describe the German soldiers? (pp. 18-19)

What do you think Charlotte is thankful for this Thanksgiving? (pp. 22-23)

Why does Charlotte hate her sister Ruth? (pp. 26-28)

What foreign language might the sailors be speaking? Why does Charlotte feel guilty for following them? (pp. 28-30)

Why do you think Charlotte's mother was upset when Charlotte says she would like many relatives? (pp. 31-33)

Is Mr. Barker a good teacher? Why or why not? (pp. 33-35)

Who do you think Mary Pickford was? (pp. 35-36)

Charlotte says that stores are allowed to sell canned vegetables again. Why would they not have been allowed to sell them?

In what way(s) would having a twin be better than having a best friend? (p. 36)

How does Charlotte describe the special relationship she has with her twin? (pp. 38-39)

What is Solomon Gundy? Make up some names for some of your favourite dishes. (pp. 39-40)

Why do you think Charlotte's parents are so mysterious about her mother's family? (p. 44)

What are "war trophies"? Why would there be an exhibition of these things? (pp. 45-49)

Charlotte describes herself as meek. Is she? What about her friend Eva? (pp. 45-53)

What do you think Charlotte and Duncan mean by "intrepidous"? (pp. 54-55)

Sometimes authors give readers a clue or hint about something that will happen later in the story. This is called "foreshadowing." When Duncan tells Charlotte his memory of the real "dragon man," could this be foreshadowing? What do you think might happen later in the story? (pp. 58-59)

Who are the "smart ones"? The young men who are fighting overseas, or those who refused to join the armed forces? Why? (pp. 59-60)

What do Charlotte and Duncan collect to put in the soldiers' Christmas stockings? What would you put in? (pp. 64-65)

What are Victory Bonds? Why would they have a school assembly about them? (pp. 66-67)

Should Duncan and Charlotte tell their parents about Ruth's plans? (p. 75)

Why would school start later in the winter? (p. 82)

What do the sayings that the Blackburn family shares mean? (pp. 82-83)

The Halifax explosion happened on December 6. How does the author deal with this day in Charlotte's diary? Is it realistic that a girl like Charlotte would have been writing in a diary in hospital on that day? Why does the author include this? (pp. 87-93)

The aftermath of the explosion

❧ What do you think has happened to the rest of Charlotte's family? (p. 95)

❧ How do the people of Halifax help each other in the days immediately following the explosion? (pp. 95-98)

❧ So far, who among Charlotte's family, friends and acquaintances has died? Who has survived? (pp. 98-100)

❧ Compare and contrast Charlotte's composition about the events of December 6 with the accounts and memories of real-life survivors of the tragedy. How does the author use real information about the events in Charlotte's account? What did she have to imagine in order to bring Charlotte's story to life? (pp. 101-111)

Two views looking south show the damage done.

❧ What do you think has happened to Duncan? (pp. 114-115)

❧ Where does Charlotte go after she's released from the hospital? (pp. 117-119)

❧ What do the survivors have to do in the days following the explosion? What kind of help do they get? (pp. 120-129)

❧ Who are the Kesslers? Why would they take so many children in? (pp. 131-134)

❧ Before reading Duncan's story, make some predictions about what you think happened to him. After reading his story, were your predictions correct? (pp. 138-140)

❧ Draw a quick sketch of one of Duncan's "superheroes," such as Duncan the Fearless, Charlotte the Brave or Matthew the Mighty. (pp. 140-141)

❧ How did the Kesslers, and Charlotte, make sure the younger children had a good Christmas? (pp. 142-146)

In what ways are the people at the Kesslers' a family? (pp. 150-151)

What surprise does Charlotte find in her diary? (p. 152)

What letters did Charlotte and Duncan find? Should they open them? (pp. 153-156)

The Kesslers, like many other families, took in children who were orphaned in the explosion, but only temporarily. What will happen to the other children at the Kesslers' with Charlotte and Duncan? (pp. 158-159)

Who is the Dragon Man? (pp. 161-164)

What challenges will Charlotte and Duncan face living with their grandparents? How is their grandparents' house different from their old one? How have their lives changed? (pp. 166-169)

Why didn't Charlotte's mother ever talk about her parents? Why did Charlotte need to know? (pp. 170-172)

How long after the explosion were the last unidentified dead buried? (pp. 176-177)

How do Charlotte, Duncan and Luke cope with their grief? How do they comfort each other? (pp. 180-184)

Luke is surprised at the rebuilding that's already going on in the Richmond area of Halifax. How long has it been since the explosion? (p. 187)

What does their father's saying mean about Luke? Why are they thinking about this before he heads back to war? (pp. 189-191)

Charlotte goes to school at the Halifax Ladies College. How long has it been since she's been to school? What does she mean when she says she's not the same Charlotte? (pp. 198-199)

Why does Charlotte decide to leave HLC and attend Tower Road School instead? (p. 201)

In what ways does Charlotte say the explosion changed her (pp. 202-203)? Use your notes to complete the reproducible on page 34.

Before reading the Epilogue, predict what will happen to Charlotte and her friends and family. What do you think she will be when she grows up?

෴ After reading the ending, decide if you think it is a good one. Are you surprised by Charlotte's choice of career? Why or why not?

——•— Extended Activities —•——

- Throughout the diary, keep track of all the things the characters do to help the war effort.

- Charlotte mentions early in her diary that while she likes to write, her twin brother Duncan likes to draw. Pretend you are Duncan and draw some of the scenes Charlotte describes vividly, such as:
  - Charlotte going on the milk wagon with Haggerty (pp. 10-11)
  - Charlotte in her velveteen dress (p. 74)
  - The aftermath of the explosion (pp. 105-106)
  - Christmas at the Kesslers' (p. 146)
  - Duncan's and Charlotte's first look at the Wakefields' house (pp. 166-167)

- Charlotte mentions many songs in her diary and many of the characters play musical instruments. Present a scene from the diary as if it were a scene from a musical theatre version of the diary, or create a story theatre version of one scene and choose appropriate background music for a soundtrack. One good scene would be seeing Luke off (p. 196). Use the reproducible on page 35 to plan your scene.

- Find out more about John McCrae, Robert Service and other Canadian poets who served during World War I. Memorize their poems and have an afternoon recitation, perhaps as a fundraiser for your favourite charity. Consider presenting some of the songs Charlotte mentions in the diary also.

- Charlotte and her friends like to write limericks. Write a limerick about Charlotte or one of her friends or family members.

- Duncan gives Charlotte a brief account of his experience, but he does not really talk about what happened to him during and after the explosion. Write or draw his version of the events of December 6 until his reunion with Charlotte on December 22.

- Charlotte is profoundly changed by the Halifax explosion, inside and outside. Create a poster that illustrates these changes using the reproducible provided on page 34.

Growing with Charlotte

Charlotte is changed by her experiences in the Halifax explosion. Create a poster that illustrates how and why she changes.

Directions:

1. Find three separate passages in the diary that show how Charlotte changes or grows.
   - Passage One: Where Charlotte started. What is she like? What are her worries?
   - Passage Two: An event that challenges and changes Charlotte.
   - Passage Three: What Charlotte is like at the end of the diary.

2. Divide your poster paper into three sections (as below) to represent the changes in Charlotte. Copy a passage from the diary into each section and illustrate it.

3. Share your poster with the rest of the class, explaining why you chose the passages you did. (Teacher: Discuss why students might have chosen different aspects of Charlotte's character to focus on.)

Frame for poster:

(Passage from diary)   (Illustration)

In the Beginning	
Life-changing Event	
At the End	

Planning a Scene

Your scene from *No Safe Harbour* should include a narrator and actors. The narrator can tell the story while the actors mime, or your scene could include both narration and dialogue among the actors. Use simple costumes, props and appropriate music for your soundtrack.

Which scene from the diary will you act out? _____

_____

_____

Pages: _____

Narrator: Played by:

_____   _____

Characters:

_____   _____

_____   _____

_____   _____

_____   _____

_____   _____

What costumes and props will you use? Where will you get them? Do you have to make them? Who will be responsible for organizing this?

_____

_____

_____

What songs would fit well in your scene? Where will you find recordings of these songs? Where will the song(s) be placed in the scene? Who will be responsible for finding the songs?

_____

_____

_____

NO SAFE HARBOUR

THE HALIFAX EXPLOSION DIARY OF CHARLOTTE BLACKBURN

—•— Bibliography —•—

Non-fiction

Airth, Lesley Anne. (2004). *What We Remember*. Ashton, ON: Maxi Pub.

Brewster, Hugh. (2006). *At Vimy Ridge: Canada's Greatest World War I Victory*. Toronto: Scholastic Canada Ltd.

Kirk, Dylan. (2004). *Canada at War*. Calgary: Weigl Educational Publishers.

Livesey, Robert. (2006). *The Great War*. Markham, ON: Fitzhenry & Whiteside Publishing.

Macleod, Elizabeth. (2007). *The Kids Book of Canada At War*. Toronto: Kids Can Press.

Fiction

Beveridge, Cathy. (2004). *Chaos in Halifax*. Vancouver: Ronsdale Press.

Haworth-Attard, Barbara. (2002). *Irish Chain*. Toronto: Harper Trophy Canada.

McKay, Sharon E. (2001). *Penelope: Terror in the Harbour*. Toronto: Penguin Books.

Background Information for Teachers

Flemming, David B. (2004). *Explosion in Halifax Harbour: The Illustrated Account of a Disaster that Shook the World*. Halifax, NS: Formac Publishing.

Frost, Leslie M. (2007). *The Wartime Letters of Leslie and Cecil Frost, 1915-1919*. Waterloo, ON: Wilfrid Laurier University Press.

Kitz, Janet F. and Payzant, Joan. (2006). *December 1917: Re-visiting the Halifax Explosion*. Halifax, NS: Nimbus Publishing.

Kitz, Janet F. (2000). *Survivors : Children of the Halifax Explosion*. Halifax, NS: Nimbus Publishing.

MacDonald, Laura. (2005). *Curse of the Narrows*. Toronto: Harper Collins.

Morton, Desmond. (1993). *When Your Number's Up: The Canadian Soldier in the First World War*. Toronto: Random House of Canada.

Tennyson, B.D. (2007). *Percy Willmot: A Cape Bretoner at War, 1914-1919*. Sydney, NS: Cape Breton University Press.

Websites

http://museum.gov.ns.ca/mma/AtoZ/halexpl
—Maritime Museum of the Atlantic, The Halifax Explosion

http://www.gov.ns.ca/nsarm/virtual/explosion
—Nova Scotia Archives and Records Management, A Vision of Regeneration

http://www.collectionscanada.gc.ca/firstworldwar
—Library and Archives Canada, Canada and the First World War

http://www.collectionscanada.gc.ca/education/firstworldwar
—Section on the Halifax Explosion, Tragedy on the Home Front

http://www.cbc.ca/halifaxexplosion
—CBC, The Halifax Explosion

TV documentaries

Shattered City: The Halifax Explosion

Canadian Experience - City of Ruins: The Halifax Explosion

Available from the Canadian Broadcasting Corporation, CBC Educational Sales at 1-866-999-3072 or email cbc_education@cbc.ca.

Canada: A People's History, Episode 12 (Ordeal by Fire 1915 – 1929)

TURNED AWAY
The World War II Diary of Devorah Bernstein

Winnipeg, Manitoba, 1941

by Carol Matas

Summary: By December 1941 Canada has been at war for over two years. Devorah Bernstein lives in Winnipeg and she is worried about her brothers who are in the Canadian Armed Forces, and she is particularly concerned about her cousin. Like Devorah's family, Sarah's family is Jewish but they are living in Paris, France, which is occupied by the German army. Though Devorah continues to play with friends, enjoy the movies and live the life of most eleven-year-olds in Canada, she follows the news about the Winnipeg Grenadiers who are stationed in Asia, and the RCAF pilots (like her brother Adam) who are stationed in Britain and flying dangerous missions into German-occupied territory in Europe. Devorah and her parents do what they can for the war effort and lobby the Canadian government to allow Jewish refugees in Canada. As Devorah learns more about the war and the treatment of the Jews at home and abroad, she also becomes involved in efforts to educate other young people about the dangers of prejudice and discrimination.

What's Going On in the World in 1941 and 1942?

— Popular films include Alfred Hitchcock's *Suspicion*, John Ford's *How Green Was My Valley*, Walt Disney's *Bambi*, and *Holiday Inn*, starring Bing Crosby.

— Clothes rationing begins in Britain.

— Enrico Fermi splits the atom.

— Popular songs include "Chattanooga Choo-Choo," "White Christmas," "Paper Doll" and "That Old Black Magic."

— The world's first working programmable computer is developed in the United States.

Prior Knowledge

The Historical Note at the end of the diary provides important background information about Nazi Germany and its anti-Semitic policies, World War II and the impact of the war on Canada. It also provides an explanation for the refusal of the Canadian government to allow the Jewish refugees into Canada and the impact of that decision on the Jewish population of Europe.

Before the reading, students could be divided into small groups to conduct some research on topics in the diary, such as: the lives of Jews in Nazi-occupied territories; the work of the Canadian Jewish Congress; Canadian troops in Europe; Canadian troops in the Pacific; and life on the home front during World War II. They could share their findings with the class.

Discussion Questions

Before commencing the reading, ask students questions that will help them make some predictions about the story.

• By 1941 Canada has been at war for several years. What was life like for the people in Canada? How did the war abroad affect the people on the home front? What is the significance of the title, *Turned Away*?

✎ Why would the author begin the diary with Sarah's letter? What background information does it give us about Devorah's and Sarah's families? How does it set the scene for the story? Begin a family tree for Devorah's extended family. (pp. 3-6)

✎ What is the Canadian Jewish Congress doing to convince the Canadian government to allow Jewish refugees from German-occupied Europe into Canada? (pp. 7-9)

✎ Why is Devorah now so worried about her brother Morris? What have you learned about Canadian soldiers in Hong Kong from Morris's letter? What do you think "fifth columnists" are? (pp. 9-13)

✎ Why do you think Devorah would feel more at home in the north end of Winnipeg? (p. 15)

✎ Where is Devorah's brother Adam? (pp. 15-18)

Winnipeg Grenadiers leaving for Hong Kong, October 25, 1941

꿎 What is the difference between the north and south ends of Winnipeg? (pp. 18-19)

꿎 Why is Devorah's class making a quilt? (pp. 19-20)

꿎 Add more information to Devorah's family tree about her aunt, uncle, cousins and grandmother. (pp. 26-27)

꿎 Why would Devorah's mother invite two airmen to their home? (p. 32)

꿎 Does Devorah do the right thing to write to Agatha Christie about her remarks about Jews? Or is Marcie right that she should just ignore them? (pp. 32-35)

꿎 What is Devorah's family's reaction when they find out that the Canadians surrendered to the Japanese at Hong Kong? Why? (pp. 37-42)

Airmen with their baggage disembark from the train at Carberry, Manitoba.

꿎 What kinds of things is Devorah already doing to keep her New Year's resolution to "make a difference"? What kinds of things do other members of the family, such as her mother, do? (pp. 42-45)

꿎 Do you think the packages Devorah and her family send to Sarah's family get to them? (pp. 47-49)

꿎 Why is Devorah having nightmares about Nazis coming to her house? (pp. 52-56)

꿎 Why did Devorah put only a little sugar in her oatmeal cookies? (pp. 57-58)

꿎 Sarah tells Devorah that her mother lets them keep small amounts of sweets. What does she usually do with them? What do you think the "black market" is? (p. 58)

꿎 Why is Devorah ashamed of her actions during If Day? Why would Winnipeg have staged If Day? How would you react to the events of that day? Would you be like Devorah or like Joe? Why? (pp. 59-62)

꿎 What do you think has happened to Morris and Adam? (pp. 65-67)

꿎 Why doesn't Devorah's mother want her and her friends to speak to the Premier about helping Sarah's and other Jewish families out of Europe? Why don't they know for sure about the Nazi concentration camps? (pp. 70-72)

❧ Devorah still goes to the movies and skates with her friends and lives a "normal" life. But in what ways is her life affected by the fact that Canada is at war (p. 73)? Keep a list of all the ways her life is affected by the war.

❧ Find out more about the work of Canadian pilots in the Royal Canadian Air Force during World War II. Is Adam's adventure in France realistic? In what ways has Carol Matas integrated real historical facts into his adventure? What do you think she made up? (pp. 76-80)

❧ What is Adam's advice to Devorah? (p. 80)

❧ Why is Devorah so happy about her weekend? What have she and her friends decided to do? (pp. 82-84)

❧ Devorah has some important conversations with her father. What lessons is she learning from him? (pp. 86-92)

An RAF plane taking part in the raid on Dieppe

❧ Why do Devorah and her friends think putting up other flags at their school is important? (pp. 95-99)

❧ Why do you think there were far more "yes" votes for conscription in English Canada than in Québec? (p. 105)

❧ Why are the Mishimas being sent from Vancouver to a farm near Brandon? (p. 106)

❧ Why is Devorah ashamed that she was upset about her fall during the dance recital? (pp. 110-113)

❧ What did Devorah learn during her flight with Adam? (pp. 122-125)

❧ Find out what "Zionism" means. Why would Devorah's parents send her to the camp? (pp. 127-129)

❧ Was Devorah's and her mother's trip worthwhile? (pp. 140-145)

❧ Do you think Morris is telling his family the truth in his letter? Why or why not? (pp. 147-148)

❧ What do you think is going to happen to Sarah? (pp. 148-151)

✎ Why would the newspaper say that Dieppe was a success for the Canadians? (p. 153)

✎ Devorah tries to make sense of many sad and bad things that happen. She asks her father, mother and brother a lot of serious questions. How do they explain these sad events to her? How do they make sense of evil? What does Devorah resolve at the end? (pp. 156-165)

The bodies of Canadian soldiers lie among damaged landing craft and tanks at Dieppe.

✎ Before reading the Epilogue, predict what will happen to Devorah and her friends and family. What do you think she will be when she grows up?

✎ After reading the ending, decide if you think this is a good ending.

—•— Extended Activities —•—

• Create a newspaper with the information and events mentioned in the diary. Remember to go back through the diary to find information to include. What movies does Devorah mention? What books does she read? These could be the basis of reviews or advertisements in the paper. What events does she talk about that could become news feature stories? Consider including stories about the war, such as the fall of Hong Kong or the Dieppe raid, as well as events in Winnipeg such as If Day. What does Devorah have strong opinions about that could be the basis of editorial or opinion pages? Are there issues that she mentions that could be the basis for letters in an advice column? Use the reproducible on page 43 to plan your newspaper.

• Pretend you are Devorah and use the reproducible on page 44 to write a wish or prayer poem.

• Devorah's mother reminds her that "many people are fighting this evil" (p. 136). Create a web or chart that shows what each member of Devorah's family is doing to fight evil.

• Is Devorah a good citizen? What is she doing that demonstrates her good citizenship? What attitudes or beliefs does she have that reflect good citizenship? Pretend you are nominating Devorah for a good citizenship award and use evidence (specific quotes) from the diary to support your nomination.

- Find out more about some of the people in Canadian history who are involved in the events Devorah mentions in her diary, such as:
  - Prime Minister William Lyon Mackenzie King
  - Lieutenant-General A.G.L. McNaughton
  - Frederick Blair
  - Cairine Wilson
  - George "Buzz" Beurling
  - Georges and Pauline Vanier

- Canada had one of the worst records of Jewish refugee resettlement in the world during and after World War II. Yet we think of Canada as a place that welcomes immigrants and refugees. Do some research into Canada's immigration history and policies after World War II. In what ways did the Canadian government learn from its mistakes regarding Jewish refugees during the war? In what ways did Canada's immigration policies remain racist or unfair?

Prime Minister William Lyon Mackenzie King

Planning a Newspaper

Preparation:

Do a scavenger hunt through a newspaper to review the parts of a newspaper. This will be a good review before you begin to plan your *Turned Away* newspaper. Cut out an example of each of the following items from your newspaper:

- Headline
- Lead story
- Index
- Editorial
- Feature story

- Advice column
- Classified ad
- Movie review
- Obituary

Activity:

Work in a group to create a newspaper for *Turned Away*. It should focus on the characters, events and time period of the diary. Include as many actual parts of a newspaper as possible. Some sample topics are included for you in italics.

Advertisements:
For the White House restaurant

Lead Story:
If Day in Winnipeg

News Feature:
Interview with Adam

Letters to the Editor:
How to help the war effort

Obituaries:
For Sarah

Cartoons:

Reviews:
Dumbo

News stories:
The Dieppe raid

Editorial:
Should Canada bring in Jewish refugees?

Advice Column:

Recipes:
Desserts using little sugar

Classified:

Name _____

A Wish or Prayer Poem

Devorah has many wishes, dreams, hopes and worries that she expresses in her diary. Skim through *Turned Away* to find words and phrases that could be included in a wish or prayer poem. Below is an example of a poem that her cousin Sarah might create:

Sarah's words or phrases:
walking on the soft sand of Winnipeg Beach   corned beef sandwiches at Oscar's
we must not give up hope   citizens of Canada   sleep
safety   delicious sweets   smelling spring in the air   get us out
someone cares for us   run freely   fear   pity
play piano   hug friends   feel warmth   laugh out loud

Sarah's prayer poem:
I pray
That one day
We will live without fear
We will feel the warm sun
And run and laugh with our friends
One day we will smell spring in the air
And find safety
And laughter
At home in Canada

Brainstorm words and phrases that represent Devorah's worries, wishes, hopes and dreams:

_____

_____

_____

_____

Write Devorah's prayer poem here:

_____   _____

_____   _____

_____   _____

_____   _____

TURNED AWAY
The World War II Diary of Devorah Bernstein

—·— Bibliography —·—

Non-fiction
Granfield, Linda. (1999). *High Flight: A Story of World War II.* Toronto: McClelland & Stewart Young Readers.

Hodge, Deborah. (2006). *The Kids Book of Canadian Immigration.* Toronto: Kids Can Press.

Hughes, Susan. (2005). *Coming to Canada: Building a Life in a New Land.* Toronto: Maple Tree Press.

Kacer, Kathy. (2006). *Hiding Edith: A True Story.* Toronto: Second Story Press.

Kirk, Dylan. (2004). *Canada At War.* Calgary: Weigl Educational Publishers.

Macleod, Elizabeth. (2007). *The Kids Book of Canada At War.* Toronto: Kids Can Press.

Fiction
Kacer, Kathy. (2003). *Margit: Home Free.* Toronto: Penguin Canada.

Kacer, Kathy. (1999). *The Secret of Gabi's Dresser.* Toronto: Second Story Press.

Matas, Carol. (2007). *The Whirlwind.* Vancouver: Orca Book Publishers.

McDonough, Yona Zeldis. (2005). *The Doll with the Yellow Star.* New York: Henry Holt and Company.

Oberman, Sheldon (1997). *By the Hanukkah Light.* Honesdale, PA: Boyds Mills Press.

Background Information for Teachers
Abella, Irving, and Troper, Harold. (2000). *None Is Too Many: Canada and the Jews of Europe, 1933-1948.* 3rd ed. Toronto: Key Porter.

Copp, Terry. (1996). *No Price Too High: Canadians and the Second World War.* Toronto: McGraw Hill Ryerson.

Granatstein, J.L. (2005). *The Last Good War: An Illustrated History of Canada in the Second World War, 1939-1945.* Vancouver: Douglas & McIntyre.

Knowles, Valerie. (2007). *Strangers at Our Gates: Canadian Immigration and Immigration Policy, 1550-2006.* Rev. ed. Toronto: Dundurn Press.

Websites
http://www.vac-acc.gc.ca/remembers
—Canadians in Hong Kong, Canadians in Asia, The Second World War, History, Veterans Affairs Canada

http://www.vac-acc.gc.ca/remembers
—The British Commonwealth Air Training Plan, The Second World War, History, Veterans Affairs Canada

http://www.wwii.ca
—Canada at War

http://www.collectionscanada.gc.ca/faces-of-war
—Faces of War, Library and Archives Canada

http://www.collectionscanada.gc.ca/military
—Second World War in From Colony to Country: A Reader's Guide to Canadian Military History, Library and Archives Canada

http://history.cbc.ca/history
—Canada: A People's History, Episode 13 (Hard Times 1929 – 1940), particularly the section on the Rise of the Fascists

TV documentaries
Canada: A People's History, Vol. 13: Hard Times (1929-1940)
Canada: A People's History, Vol. 14: The Crucible (1940-1946)
Historica Minutes, Pauline Vanier. Available at Histori.ca

— Giving Gifts —

In *No Safe Harbour* Charlotte says that she'd like to send her brother Luke, serving overseas with the Canadian army, a box of sleep (p. 17). Create three gifts for the character(s) of your choice from a Dear Canada diary. You can give one character three gifts or distribute them to different characters. Gifts can be real things or "intangible" things, like Charlotte's gift of sleep.

Draw each gift inside a box, with a tag that identifies who the gift is for, and that explains why the gift was given. What makes this an appropriate and meaningful gift for the character?

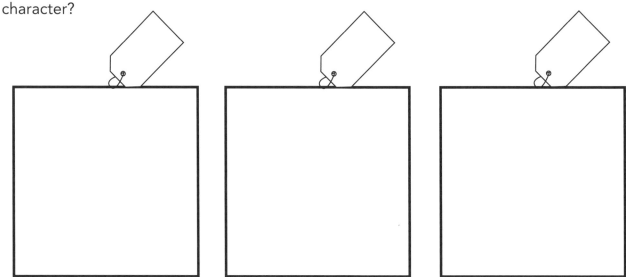

— Word Wall —

Create a word wall to record interesting and unusual vocabulary from the diary. For example, under "V" might be "Victrola" from *No Safe Harbour*.

AB	C	D	E
FG	H	IJ	KL
M	NO	P	QR
S	T	UVW	XYZ

Name _____

— Character Map —

Trait: _____

Evidence: _____

_____
_____
_____
_____
_____
_____
_____
_____
_____
_____
_____

Trait: _____

Evidence: _____

_____
_____
_____
_____
_____
_____
_____
_____
_____
_____
_____

Trait: _____

Evidence: _____

_____
_____
_____
_____
_____
_____
_____
_____
_____
_____
_____

Trait: _____

Evidence: _____

_____
_____
_____
_____
_____
_____
_____
_____
_____
_____
_____

Photo Credits

Page 7: Library and Archives Canada, C-006217

Page 10: Library and Archives Canada, Acc. No. 1972-26-778; Library and Archives Canada, Acc. No. 1972-26-1382

Page 11: Library and Archives Canada, C-001080

Page 13: Library and Archives Canada, Acc. No. R9266-1109 Peter Winkworth Collection of Canadiana

Page 18: Library and Archives Canada, Acc. No. 1961-29(34)

Page 19: Library and Archives Canada, Acc. No. 1972-26-1385

Page 20: Library and Archives Canada, Acc. No. 1990-553-743

Page 23: Library and Archives Canada, Acc. No. 1996-115-1; Library and Archives Canada, Acc. No. R9266-3154 Peter Winkworth Collection of Canadiana

Page 28: Library and Archives Canada, C-003624A

Page 30: W.G. MacLaughlan, Library and Archives Canada, C-017501 (cropped)

Page 31: Library and Archives Canada, C-019944; W.G. MacLaughlan, Library and Archives Canada, C-019948

Page 38: Dept. of National Defence, Library and Archives Canada, PA-161202

Page 39: Western Canadian Pictorial Index, A0641 – 19763

Page 40: Library and Archives Canada, PA-183771

Page 41: Library and Archives Canada, C-014160

Page 42: Yousef Karsh, Library and Archives Canada, C-027650

Back cover: B. Wirzba

Library and Archives Canada Cataloguing in Publication

Von Heyking, Amy J. (Amy Jeanette), 1965-
  Teaching with Dear Canada : build important social studies and
language skills with historical fiction. Vol. 4 / by Amy von Heyking.
(Dear Canada)
Includes bibliographical references.
ISBN 978-0-545-99414-9

  1. English language—Study and teaching (Elementary). 2. Children's
stories, Canadian (English)—Study and teaching (Elementary).
3. Canada—History—Study and teaching (Elementary). 4. Social
sciences—Study and teaching (Elementary). 5. Canadian diaries
(English)—Study and teaching (Elementary). I. Title. II. Series.
PS8039.F5V655 2008   372.64'044   C2007-907190-2

ISBN-10 0-545-99414-4

6 5 4 3 2 1   Printed in Canada   08 09 10 11 12 13